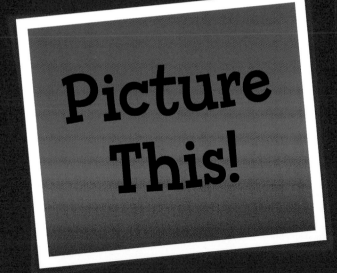

Picture This!

Festivals

Rebecca Rissman

Raintree

Raintree is an imprint of Capstone Global Library Limited, a company incorporated in England and Wales having its registered office at 7 Pilgrim Street, London, EC4V 6LB – Registered company number: 6695582

www.raintreepublishers.co.uk
myorders@raintreepublishers.co.uk

Text © Capstone Global Library Limited 2014
First published in hardback in 2014
First published in paperback in 2015
The moral rights of the proprietor have been asserted.

Edited by Daniel Nunn, Catherine Veitch, and Clare Lewis
Designed by Marcus Bell
Picture research by Liz Alexander
Production by Victoria Fitzgerald
Originated by Capstone Global Library Ltd
Printed and bound in China

ISBN 978 1 406 25964 3 (hardback)
17 16 15 14 13
10 9 8 7 6 5 4 3 2 1

ISBN 978 1 406 25969 8 (paperback)
18 17 16 15 14
10 9 8 7 6 5 4 3 2 1

British Library Cataloguing in Publication Data
A full catalogue record for this book is available from the British Library.

Acknowledgements

We would like to thank the following for permission to reproduce photographs: Corbis pp. 3 (© Abed Rahim Khatib/Demotix), 15 (© Abed Rahim Khatib/Demotix); Dreamstime pp. 3 (© Lucidwaters), 17 (© Lucidwaters); Getty Images pp. 5 (Leland Bobbe/Photonica), 14 (Noah Seelam/AFP); iStockphhoto pp. 3 (© Kulpreet_Photography), 12 (© desifoto), 13 (© Kulpreet_Photography); Shutterstock pp. 3 (© Cherkas, © Filip Fuxa, © kaczor58, © Shaiith, © wavebreakmedia), 4 (© Cherkas, © Bikeworldtravel, © DanielW, © manzrussali, © WH CHOW), 5 (© fotohunter, © Norman Chan, © Christophe Testi), 6 (© Filip Fuxa, © Terrie L. Zeller, © photofriday), 7 (© Yuri Arcurs), 8 (© Monkey Business Images, © Calek, pryzmat, © margouillat photo, © kaczor58, © Ruth Black), 9 (© spirit of America, © Martin Dallaire, © jorisvo), 10 (© 9246263575, © Monkey Business Images, © Shaiith, © Daniel Schweinert), 11 (© dragon_fang, © Vidux, © Monkey Business Images, © My Good Images, © DenisNata), 12 (© silentwings, © D.Shashikant), 14 (© hainaultphoto, © JOAT, © AJP), 16 (© Scott Rothstein, © ChameleonsEye, © iPixela, © ChameleonsEye), 18 (© Alexander Hoffmann, © Hannamariah, © Victorian Traditions, © Konrad Mostert), 19 (© wavebreakmedia), 23 (© Christophe Testi).

Front cover photograph of fireworks over Central Park on New Year's Eve in New York City reproduced with permission of Getty Images (Daniel A Ferrara/Flickr).

Back cover photographs of a family celebrating Hanukkah reproduced with permission of Dreamstime (© Lucidwaters).

Every effort has been made to contact copyright holders of material reproduced in this book. Any omissions will be rectified in subsequent printings if notice is given to the publisher.

Contents

New Year 4

Valentine's day 6

Easter 8

Halloween. 10

Diwali 12

Ramadan 14

Hanukkah. 16

Christmas. 18

Find out more about the photos. . . . 20

Discussion questions. 22

Index 24

New Year

Valentine's Day

Easter

Halloween

Diwali

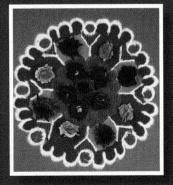

Ramadan

Hanukkah

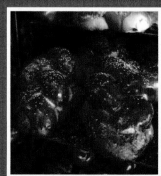

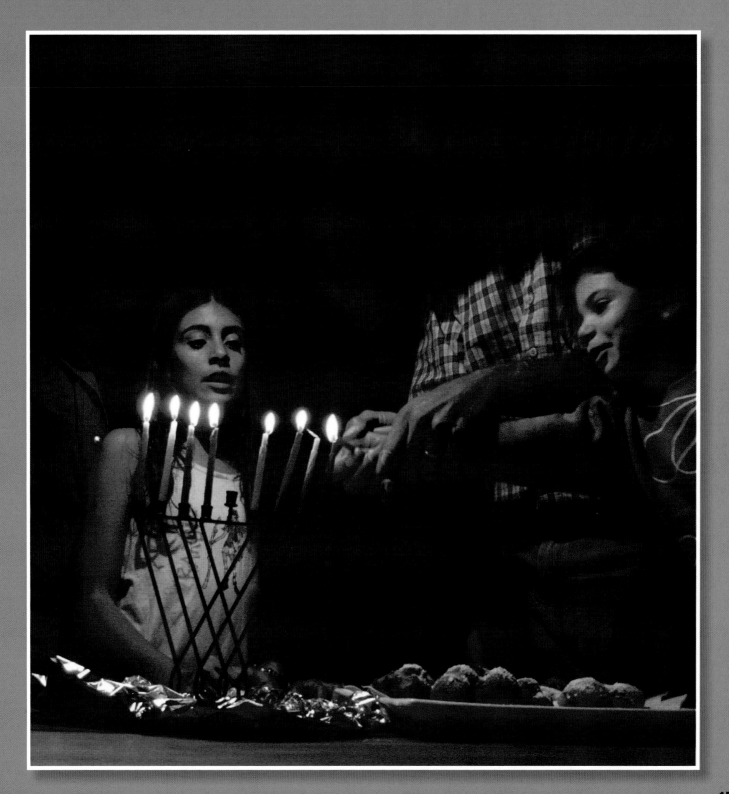

Christmas

Find out more about the photos

Page 4 Photos on this page show New Year's Eve fireworks in Times Square, New York, and London, England.

Page 5 The photos of red lanterns, red envelopes, and a dancing dragon show Chinese New Year being celebrated. In the top right photo, party goers celebrate the New Year in the United States.

Page 6 The red roses pictured at the top of this page are a symbol of Valentine's Day. The bottom centre and bottom left photos show Valentine's Day cards. At the bottom right, a bouquet of pink roses is arranged in the shape of a heart to celebrate the day.

Page 7 This photo shows a florist making an arrangement of flowers for a Valentine's Day customer.

Page 8 Painted, dyed, and chocolate eggs are symbols of Easter. This page shows eggs from around the world that have been decorated, or given as gifts to celebrate Easter.

Page 9 The top photo shows an actor portraying Jesus Christ in an Easter parade in California, USA. At the bottom left, a photo shows a woman in New York wearing a special hat to an Easter parade. The photo at the bottom right shows a stained-glass window in a church in Stockholm, Sweden.

Page 10 Two photos at the top of this page show children dressed in festive Halloween costumes. The photos at the top right and bottom of this page show carved Halloween pumpkins.

Page 11 At the top left of this page, two photos show children reading spooky stories. The three large photos show children dressed in Halloween costumes.

Page 12 The photo at the top of this page shows an Indian woman's hands that have been decorated in beautiful henna designs. In the bottom left corner, a photo shows a box of baked sweets. The photos at the bottom centre and right show beautiful Diwali rangoli. Rangoli are traditional folk art designs made on the floor during Hindu festivals.

Page 13 Diwali lamps shine beautifully in this large photo.

Page 14 The top photo on this page shows a Koran and prayer beads. In the bottom left corner, a photo shows two Indian Muslim boys greeting each other during Ramadan. The bottom centre photo shows a Ramadan lamp shining brightly. In the bottom right corner, a Muslim man prays during Ramadan.

Page 15 A Muslim girl in Palestine carries a lantern during Ramadan in this photo.

Page 16 The photo at the top of this page shows a Hebrew Bible and dreidel. The photos at the bottom of the page show different foods enjoyed during Hanukkah: sufgniyot, cookies in the shape of the Star of David, and challah bread. Sufganiyot are jam or cream doughnuts that are traditionally eaten in the days leading up to Hannukah.

Page 17 This photo shows a family lighting a candle on the menorah to celebrate Hanukkah.

Page 18 The photo at the top of this page shows a porcelain nativity scene. In the bottom left corner, a photo shows a house decorated in Christmas lights. The bottom centre photo shows a drawing of Father Christmas carrying a bag of gifts. In the bottom right photo, a couple celebrates Christmas at the beach in Australia.

Page 19 This page shows a photo of a family decorating a Christmas tree with lights and ornaments.

Discussion questions

Pages 4–5 show New Year celebrations from around the world. Three images on page 5 show Chinese New Year celebrations. Chinese New Year is usually in January or February and is the most important holiday in the Chinese calendar.

How do you celebrate New Year?

Why is New Year's Eve a special day?

Pages 6–7 show different Valentine's Day symbols and traditions.

What do you do on Valentines Day?

What colours do you think of on Valentine's Day?

Pages 8–9 show different Easter symbols and traditions. Christians celebrate Easter in the Spring.

Can you think of any other Easter symbols?

Do you celebrate Easter?

What animals are associated with Easter?

Pages 10–11 show photos of children dressed in Halloween costumes and carved pumpkins.

Can you think of any other Halloween symbols?

What do you like to do at Halloween?

Have you ever carved a pumpkin?

Have you ever been trick-or-treating?

Pages 12–13 feature photos of Diwali symbols, such as lanterns and sweets. Diwali is the Hindu festival of light.

Can you think of any other symbols of this festival?

Pages 14–15 show photos of Ramadan symbols and traditions. Muslim people recognize Ramadan in the ninth month of the Islamic calendar.

The Koran is the Muslim holy book. Why do you think it is a symbol for Ramadan?

Do you celebrate Ramadan?
How do you celebrate?

Pages 16–17 show photos of Hannukah symbols and traditions. Jewish people celebrate Hannukah in the autumn or winter. Hannukah is often called the "Festival of Lights".

Foods cooked in oil are often eaten during Hannukah.

Can you think of any other foods that are symbols of Hannukah?

Do you celebrate Hannukah?
How do you celebrate?

What shape are the biscuits on the bottom of page 16?

Pages 18–19 show photos of Christmas symbols and traditions. Christian people celebrate Christmas on December 25th. They celebrate this as the day that Jesus Christ was born.

Father Christmas is a symbol of Christmas. Do you know any stories about Father Christmas?
Do you know another name for Father Christmas?

Do you celebrate Christmas? What special foods do you eat?

Index

beach 18
Bible 16
books 11

cake 8
challah bread 16
Chinese dragon 5
Christmas 18–19
    lights 18
    tree 19

Diwali 12–13
dreidel 16
dressing up 10–11

Easter 8-9
    parade 9
Easter hat 9
eggs 8
    painted 8
    chocolate 8

families 17, 19
fireworks 4
flowers 6–7, 9, 12
    roses 6
food 12, 16, 17

gifts 18

Halloween 10–11
Hannukkah 16–17
hearts 6
Hebrew 16
henna 12

Islam 14–15

Koran 14

lamps 12–13, 14
lanterns 5, 10, 11, 14, 15
lights 18, 19
London 4

menorah 17, 21

nativity 18
New Year 4–7
    Chinese 5

prayer beads 14
praying 14
pumpkin lanterns 10–11

Ramadan 14–15
rangoli 12

Santa Claus 18
stained-glass window 9
Star of David 16
sweets 10, 11

trick or treat 10

Valentine's Day 6–7